D0936243

Girls'

SOCCER

by Alex Monnig

GIRLS'
SportsZone

Printed in the United States of America,
North Mankato, Minnesota

052013
012014

 THIS BOOK CONTAINS AT LEAST 10% RECYCLED MATERIALS.

Editor: Chrös McDougall
Series Designer: Marie Tupy

Photo Credits: Shutterstock Images, cover, 1, 44; Petr David Josek/AP Images, 5, 26; David J. Phillip/ AP Images, 7; John G. Mabanglo/AFP/Getty Images, 9; Khaled Desouki/AFP/Getty Images, 11; Jae C. Hong/AP Images, 13; Martin Meissner/AP Images, 15; Lefteris Pitarakis/AP Images, 17; Armando Franca/AP Images, 18; Julie Jacobson/AP Images, 21; Jens Meyer/AP Images, 23; Lefteris Pitarakis/ AP Images, 25; Jamie Sabau/Getty Images, 29; Chris Clark/AP Images, 31; Kyodo/AP Images, 33; Hussein Malla/AP Images, 34; Stuart Franklin/FIFA/Getty Images, 37; Ben Curtis/AP Images, 40, 42

Library of Congress Control Number: 2013932515

Cataloging-in-Publication Data

Monnig, Alex.
 Girls' soccer / Alex Monnig.
  p. cm. -- (Girls' sportszone)
 ISBN 978-1-61783-989-4 (lib. bdg.)
 Includes bibliographical references and index.
 1. Soccer for girls--Juvenile literature. I. Title.
 796.334--dc23

                                                          2013932515

Table of Contents

chapter 1

Heading with Abby Wambach

Midfielder Megan Rapinoe dribbled the ball up the left side of the field. The fate of the United States at the 2011 Women's World Cup was at stake. Brazil led 2–1 in the second extra-time period of the quarterfinal match. Only two minutes remained. Rapinoe's American teammates charged up the field in a final, desperate attempt to tie the game.

Rapinoe planted her right foot and drove the ball with her left. It sailed toward Brazil's goal. Four defenders stood in the penalty box. But the ball flew past them toward the back post. US forward Abby Wambach was right there waiting.

The United States' Abby Wambach (20) drills a last-chance header into Brazil's goal to tie their game at the 2011 Women's World Cup.

Wambach leaped into the air, greeting the ball with her forehead. It flew past Brazil's flailing goalie and sailed into the net. In one amazing play, the game was tied. And with a penalty shootout victory a few minutes later, Team USA advanced in the tournament.

Wambach was not finished. The United States met France in the semifinal. This time Wambach scored the go-ahead goal in the 79th minute. That sent Team USA to the World Cup final for the first time since 1999.

Those goals made Wambach a national celebrity in the United States. Those who followed women's soccer were hardly surprised by her performance, though. Wambach debuted with the US team in September 2001 against Germany. She scored her first international goal less than a year later against Finland, on April 27, 2002. She has hardly slowed down since.

The goal against France was Wambach's 121st in international competition. A whopping 49 of those had been scored with her head.

"I just know that if I put my courage and my body into any ball served in the box, whether I score or not I'm going to wreak havoc with any defense," she said.

Wambach's ability to score with her head has made her one of the most dangerous scorers of all time. Through 2012, she had 152 goals. That put her on pace to someday break Mia Hamm's record of 158 goals. Wambach tied Hamm in another way that year. With Team USA's win at the 2012 Olympic Games, both Wambach and Hamm had two gold medals.

Abby Wambach (14) heads the ball past two China defenders for a goal during a game in 2012.

DIFFERENT HEADERS

Not all headers have the same purpose. A header shot needs to be hard and accurate. Usually players will aim low with header shots. Low shots are often harder to save. So players should push their head forward and downward as they drive their foreheads into the ball. Meanwhile, defensive headers usually clear the ball away from danger. That means players often aim to hit the ball higher and farther. So it is important for the player to get low. That way she can use her legs to help push upward and drive a powerful header into space.

Honing the Header

Soccer is a game played primarily with the feet. However, only the hands and arms are actually barred from touching the ball for field players. The best players can make plays with more than their feet. Often you will see a player trap or control the ball with her thighs or chest. Arguably the most important body part outside of the feet, however, is the head.

Headers are important because they allow a player to quickly hit a ball that is sailing through the air. And players can physically use their heads in many ways during a soccer game.

As Wambach has shown, headers are a great way to shoot on goal. A pass through the air is more likely to get through a crowded penalty box. Then a header can quickly change the direction of the ball. That makes a well-placed shot off the head very difficult to save.

Similarly, defensive players often need to use their heads too. They can use their heads to clear a cross or corner kick through the air. Players can also pass using headers. However, headers are more difficult to aim than a foot pass. The key for a header pass is to send the ball to a teammate's feet. The feet are the best body part for controlling the ball.

That said, headers can be dangerous. Proper technique is vital for preventing injury. The first step is positioning. A player should bend her knees and position herself to squarely connect with the ball. Then she must properly hit the ball. Her eyes should be open so she can see the ball and

Legendary US player Mia Hamm heads the ball past a Brazilian player during the 1999 Women's World Cup.

Quick Tip: Hitting the Sweet Spot

Former US women's national team coach Pia Sundhage knew what made Abby Wambach's headers so successful. "She has power and timing, and she makes life very difficult for other teams," Sundhage said. Wambach learned from a young age through a specific drill. She lies flat on her stomach, facing straight ahead, holding herself up with her elbows. Then she has somebody to sit close in front of her and toss the ball at her head. She extends her neck forward, keeping her eyes looking straight ahead. Then she meets the ball with her forehead to send it back to the person that tossed it. She makes sure to keep her neck strong and straight, rather than nodding her head up and down like she is saying "yes." The drill helps with timing the header and with contacting the ball with the forehead instead of the top of the head.

time her header. And the header should always be purposeful. The ball should not simply bounce off one's head. Rather, the player should stiffen her neck and push her head into the ball. Finally, the player should hit the ball with her forehead. This helps aim the header while also preventing injuries, such as a concussion.

Getting to Wambach's level takes lots of practice. It takes time to get used to hitting a fast-moving ball with your forehead. Then it takes even more time to learn to be accurate. Good headers are about more than technique, though. Positioning and size are also important. Wambach has a natural advantage over most players. That is because she is 5 feet,

11 inches and weighs 170 pounds. That makes her taller than some of the defenders she matches up against. Her big frame allows her to get in good positions to meet the ball with her head.

Players don't have to be tall to be good at headers, though. Any player can pass with her head in the open field. And with great instincts and positioning, even smaller players can be great shooters and defenders with their heads.

Abby Wambach (14) gets high in the air for a header against Japan during the 2012 Olympic gold-medal game in London.

chapter 2

Shooting With Alex Morgan

T he United States faced Japan in the final of the 2011 Women's World Cup. The match was scoreless at halftime. So US coach Pia Sundhage put Alex Morgan in. The 22-year-old forward had been a super substitute during the tournament. She had already scored the important third goal in a 3–1 semifinal win over France. Sundhage hoped Morgan could bring more magic to the final.

Midfielder Megan Rapinoe gathered the ball deep in US territory in the 69th minute. She then blasted the ball more than 50 yards (45.7 m) down the middle of the field. It flew past five Japan defenders.

Morgan knew that Rapinoe had a powerful leg and could launch the ball into a dangerous position. So Morgan had started sprinting down the

Alex Morgan prepares to shoot against Australia during a 2012 game.

SUPERB SUBSTITUTE

It might be hard to believe that Alex Morgan was ever a reserve player. But that is exactly what she was for much of her early career with the US national team. Morgan's first international appearance was in a game against Mexico on March 31, 2010. She was a sub in that game. She went on to play in seven more games for Team USA that year. Every time she came off the bench. Even at the 2011 Women's World Cup Morgan came in as a sub in five of her six games. She finally broke into the starting lineup for good in 2012.

field as soon as Rapinoe booted the ball. Morgan battled with the final Japan defender for position. The ball bounced once as Morgan got to the defender's inside. Morgan collected the ball on the second bounce and kept it moving forward. Then she tapped it with her right foot into the penalty box. The Japan defender was hot on Morgan's heels. But Morgan's delicate touch opened up some space to shoot.

"The goalkeeper was tall [and] leaning toward the near post," Morgan said. "I decided right away that I was going to shoot low and hard [to the] far post." So she planted her right foot next to the ball. Morgan faced her target as she gained enough balance to strike. Then she blasted a left-footed shot past the lunging goalkeeper and inside the far post. United States 1, Japan 0.

Japan eventually came back to win the match in a shootout. But with that goal, Morgan left her mark on the tournament. Now the whole world knew that the youngest player on Team USA would soon be one of the most lethal strikers in women's soccer.

That scoring prowess showed one year later in the 2012 Olympic semifinal. Morgan's goal in the 123rd minute put Team USA ahead of Canada 4–3. That sent Team USA to the gold-medal game while avoiding a shootout.

"Some players have a gift [for] scoring goals when it's most needed," Sundhage said of Morgan after the Olympic semifinal. "She continues to bring her game to every single game."

Alex Morgan (13) drills a shot that scores the opening goal against Japan during the 2011 Women's World Cup final in Germany.

Going for the Goal

There is one way to win a soccer game: score more goals than your opponent. The most common way of scoring is by shooting with the foot.

Players such as Morgan can shoot in many different ways and from many parts of the field. No matter what, there are some basic fundamentals of shooting. Most shots come off the laces of a player's shoes. That results in the most powerful shots. Balance and positioning are also important. A player shooting with her right foot should try to plant her left foot next to the ball. That sets a balanced foundation so the right leg can swing powerfully through the ball. It is also important for the shooter to face her target. This helps a shot be more accurate.

As Morgan showed in the 2011 World Cup, players often need to create the space to shoot. Morgan tapped the ball far enough away from the defender

20:20 VISION

On December 9, 2012, Alex Morgan assisted on Sydney Leroux's goal in a 2–0 win over China. That gave Morgan 20 assists for the year. It made her only the second US woman to record 20 goals and 20 assists in a single year. US legend Mia Hamm was the other. "It's really great to be in that exclusive club with Mia, someone that I looked up to for many years," Morgan said. Morgan finished the year with 28 goals and 21 assists.

so that the defender could not block it. Yet the ball was still close enough that Morgan could hit a hard, balanced shot.

Once a player has space to shoot, she must decide how hard to strike the ball. The harder the shot, the faster the goalie must react. However, powerful shots are also harder to control. Sometimes a player might have a lot of space in which to shoot. In that case, the key is a softer and more accurate shot. Other times a goalie might be standing farther out from the

Japan's Yuki Ogimi shoots for a goal against Brazil during the 2012 Olympic Games.

goal line. Then a player can try chipping the ball over her head with a soft, looping shot.

Placement is the other key factor in shooting. A player has the option of sending the ball high or low, left or right. The best option often depends both on the shooter's placement and the goalie's placement. A shot from the middle of the field gives the most possibilities. Usually the goalie will

Alex Morgan (13) shoots to score Team USA's fourth goal during a game against Iceland in the 2011 Algarve Cup championship.

Quick Tip: Straight Shooting

Alex Morgan is known for doing shooting drills during breaks in training. One shot she has practiced thousands of times is a low, hard drive. Morgan is a left-footed player. So she plants her right foot beside the ball, facing her target. When she approaches, she keeps her knee over the ball and leans her body forward. Her eyes are looking at the ball the whole time. Morgan dips her foot down to strike the ball with the laces. "That's where you're going to get the most power and the most accuracy," she said. "Typically you want to follow through with that same striking foot and land on the same foot you kicked with."

be standing in the middle of the net. So the best shot is often a hard one toward one of the corners.

It is harder to score coming in from an angle. The goalie can move to the side and cut off the angle. That leaves a smaller target at which to shoot. Morgan shot toward the outside post. Almost any coach would agree. There is more space to the outside.

Scoring on a breakaway requires a lot of skill and concentration. One way players increase their chances is by shooting low. Goalies make many saves with their hands. So higher shots are often easier to save than low shots. Shooting low is a good tactic on a close-range shot as well.

chapter 3

Dribbling with Marta

B razil's marvelous Marta was not finished toying with the US defense. The midfielder had already scored a goal in the semifinal match at the 2007 Women's World Cup in China. She had put her team up 2–0 with a low shot in the 27th minute after evading several US defenders.

Her goal late in the second half was even more masterful. By the 79th minute Brazil held a comfortable 3–0 lead. Marta received a pass on the left side of the field and deep in US territory.

Her teammate had sent the ball through the air. It bounced awkwardly a few feet in front of Marta. But it was no problem for the star playmaker.

Marta (10) evades US defenders during their semifinal game at the
2007 Women's World Cup in China.

FAMOUS FEET

Women were barred from playing organized soccer in Brazil until 1979. Even after that, many people looked down on women's soccer. Marta has done much to change that. In 2007 she helped her team win the Pan American Games. The championship was at the famous Maracana Stadium in Brazil. A ring of honor around that stadium features the footprints of many great men's players. After the game, Marta became the first woman to add her footprints to that ring.

Her skills with the ball rivaled those of anyone in the world—man or woman.

Marta began with her back to the US goal. An American defender stood right behind her. Marta met the ball on its first bounce with the inside of her right foot. The ball bounced again in front of her. Then, in a flash, she flicked it behind her with the outside of her left foot. The ball sailed over the head of the bewildered US defender, who turned for a split second to locate the ball.

That was all the time Marta needed. With lightning speed she spun around her opponent and into the penalty box. She faked out a final US defender. The defender nearly fell down because she was so fooled. Then Marta cut the ball to her left foot, contorted her body, and shot back to the near post. The ball flew into the net. It was a goal for the ages.

"If you ask me how I do that, I can't explain," Marta said. "Things happen very quickly during the match, and afterward I start thinking: 'How do I do that?'"

Opponents have been wondering the same thing since Marta burst onto the scene. Marta's strikes against the United States were just two of seven in the tournament. No player scored more goals. That scoring streak earned her the Golden Shoe for being top scorer and the Golden Ball for being the tournament's best player.

Marta, *left*, jukes past a Norway defender on her way to a goal during the 2011 Women's World Cup in Germany.

Marta had already built quite the reputation before the 2007 Women's World Cup. Brazil is famous for its soccer. The country's players have a flashy style known as *Jogo Bonito*. That is Portuguese for "the beautiful game." It focuses on fancy footwork and excellent ball control skills. Brazilian men's forward Pelé is often considered the best soccer player ever. He was at the center of Jogo Bonito's rise. So it was no small compliment when Pelé himself called Marta "Pelé in skirts." Nor was it a small feat when Marta was named the world's women's player of the year every year from 2006 to 2010.

Keeping the Ball

Dribbling is one of the most important parts of soccer. Besides passing, it is the main way the ball is moved around the field. A good touch on the ball can be the difference between beating a defender and losing the ball. It can also be the difference between creating a goal-scoring opportunity and a turnover.

To dribble a soccer ball is to control the soccer ball. This is done through a series of light touches on the ball using the feet. However, dribbling looks much different depending on the situation.

A player running down the field with the ball will tap the ball slightly harder. The key is to keep control of the ball. If the player taps the ball too hard, it becomes easier to steal. But if she taps it too softly, the player will have to slow down or risk losing the ball.

Dribbling in the short field often involves more touches. It is important for the dribbler to keep the ball close. If it sits farther away it is harder to control and easier to steal. That control becomes even more important

Brazil's Cristiane, *right*, controls the ball during a match against Japan at the 2012 Olympic Games.

when a defender gets near. The player with the ball needs to constantly keep the ball moving. If not, the defender can easily knock it away.

A player can dribble to hold onto the ball between passes. Players can also dribble to take on defenders. The key to this is in the footwork. A good dribbler can keep the defender off balance by mixing things up. This can mean tapping the ball with different parts of her feet. It can also mean tapping the ball at different speeds. For example, a player might tap the

Marta, *left*, dribbles away from a Norway defender during the 2011 Women's World Cup.

Quick Tip: Coning Your Skills

It takes a lot of practice to be able to control the ball like Marta. One of the best ways to develop quality dribbling skills is to set up cones in various formations and dribble around them. Start off easy. Set up four to five cones, each three giant steps apart from each other, in a straight line. Then dribble through them using both the outside and inside of the dominant foot. Try not to let the ball hit the cones. As you get more comfortable, switch feet. You can also move the cones closer and closer together to create tighter, more difficult spaces to dribble in.

ball three times softly and then tap it harder when making her move. The key, as always, is maintaining control.

Foot control is the most important part of dribbling. However, players such as Marta often use their bodies to try to confuse defenders. For example, a player might lower her left shoulder so the defender commits to that side. Then she will tap the ball harder to her right and break that way.

Nobody is born a great dribbler. The best players are constantly practicing and trying new moves. But dribbling doesn't have to be done in practice. It doesn't even have to be done with friends. Players can always find fun and creative ways to play with a soccer ball.

chapter 4

Passing with Megan Rapinoe

T eam USA opened the 2012 Olympic Games against France. But things could not have started much worse for the Americans. Within 14 minutes France was already up 2–0. That didn't sit well with the US players. Team USA was the defending champion. In fact, the United States had won three of the four gold medals since women's soccer was added to the Olympics in 1996. So the US players wanted to win badly in 2012.

Megan Rapinoe helped make sure that score did not stand for long. The United States was awarded a corner kick in the 19th minute. Rapinoe curled the ball toward the far post to teammate Abby Wambach. It was a perfect cross. Wambach headed it home to make the score 2–1.

Megan Rapinoe, *left*, of the United States shows great vision and technique with her passing.

ACL AGONY

Megan Rapinoe was rising through the ranks of the US women's soccer program in 2006. Then she was hit with an anterior cruciate ligament (ACL) injury. That forced her to have surgery on her knee. Then she had to regain her strength and ability to cut. Rapinoe was almost back to full health in 2007. Then she re-injured her ACL and was forced to go through it all again. She never gave up though. Soon Rapinoe was one of the most valuable players on the US women's national team.

Alex Morgan scored the game-tying goal in the 32nd minute. But the comeback was hardly over. Rapinoe pounced on a loose ball in the 56th minute and raced down the right wing. Two defenders ran to meet her. But before they could take the ball, Rapinoe slipped a perfect pass to her left. Midfielder Carli Lloyd received it just outside the center of the penalty box. She took two touches on the ball and nailed a shot from outside of the box. It sailed into the far side of the goal to put Team USA up 3–2.

Rapinoe had already helped set up two goals. She still was not done. Rapinoe had the ball near midfield at the 66th minute. Three defenders came in to contain her. But Rapinoe launched a long, bouncing pass down the field to the far left corner. It went perfectly to wide-open midfielder Tobin Heath. Heath then raced with the ball toward the goal. Just before two defenders reached her at the goal area, Heath sent a low pass across the net. Waiting at the far side was Morgan. She merely had to set the ball into the wide-open net to seal the 4–2 victory.

The headlines after the game focused around the goal scorers. But directly behind three of those goals was Rapinoe. The fun-loving midfielder from Redding, California, is easy to spot on the field. She stands out with her bleached-blonde hair. But those who look a little closer see one of the most creative offensive players in the world. Rapinoe has an eye for what is going on and what is about to happen. Then she has the skills to get the ball to the perfect spot so the play can continue.

Megan Rapinoe, *right*, and Alex Morgan celebrate after Morgan scored her goal against France at the 2012 Olympics.

Rapinoe has been on the beginning end of some of the most famous goals in US soccer history. It was Rapinoe who hit the long cross that Wambach headed in to tie Brazil in the 2011 Women's World Cup quarterfinals. It was Rapinoe who hit the long pass up the middle that Morgan used to score the opening goal against Japan in the final. And it was Rapinoe who sent a cross flying through the night sky in the dying moments of the 2012 Olympic semifinal against Canada. Wambach finished that one as well, and Team USA went on to win.

"Megan, she's one of the players on our team that has the ability to change the game," Wambach said. "She can come on and be the best player on the field."

The Perks of Passing

Passing the ball is the easiest way to move the ball. This is because passing moves the ball around the field much faster than dribbling. It is vital that any soccer team must be able to string several passes together throughout a game. A team that dribbles too much usually struggles to maintain possession.

Passing serves many purposes in soccer. One is simply to keep possession of the ball. After all, the opposing team cannot score if it doesn't have the ball. If defenders are pressuring a player, she can simply pass to an open teammate. That creates more time and space to develop an attack. Developing an attack and maintaining possession often mean

Homare Sawa, *right*, of Japan passes the ball against Canada during a match at the 2012 Olympic Games.

passing to the sides and even to the back. The objective is simply to keep the ball safe and away from the other team.

Eventually any team has to attack. Passing is usually the best way to set up an attack, too. Players without the ball in soccer should always be moving to open space. When attacking, the player with the ball often passes to an area where a teammate is running. This is called a through pass. These types of passes expose holes in the defense and can lead to scoring opportunities.

"I've never scored a goal without receiving a pass from my teammates," Wambach said.

Team USA's Megan Rapinoe, *left*, prepares to pass the ball past Canada's Christine Sinclair during the 2012 Olympic semifinals.

Quick Tip: Staying on Target

Passing is only effective if it goes to the right place, whether that is to a teammate or to an open space. There are lots of ways you can work on passing accuracy. One simple drill requires a partner and some cones. Set the two cones a few feet apart, making a "window." Stand back-to-back with your partner in the window and then take a few steps apart. Turn around and the window should be between you and your partner. Try passing the ball through the cones and to your partner. Then she passes it back. If you're doing well, try standing farther apart or putting the cones closer together.

As Rapinoe showed against France, there are many ways to get the ball to a teammate. The most common way to pass is with the inside of the foot. One foot is placed next to the ball and aimed toward the target. The other foot swings and sends the ball moving. Passes can also go through the air. These passes go farther. However, they are less accurate and harder to receive. Most of these passes are made with the inside of the laces. This is how most players take free kicks and corner kicks.

Fundamentals are important. But what sets players like Rapinoe apart is vision. Rapinoe watches her teammates. She can see where they are running and where there is open space. She knows exactly when to send the ball to that open space. As she has proven so many times, that is a recipe for success.

chapter 5

Goalkeeping with Hope Solo

American Hope Solo is known as one of the best goalkeepers in the world. So she clearly wasn't happy with her performance against Canada in the 2012 Olympic semifinal. The United States barely won by a score of 4–3. Solo knew she could do better. She knew she *had* to do better. Soccer teams can't win many games when they give up three goals.

A good goalie must have certain skills. She has to be quick. She has to have soft hands. She has to have good eyes. She has to be able to fly through the air. And she definitely needs to have a short memory. A goalie who gets scored on must quickly forget and get ready to stop the next shot.

Hope Solo stays alert and in position during a US Women's National Team game against Germany in 2012.

Solo showed that she is all of those things. Team USA met Japan in the Olympic gold-medal game. It was a rematch of the Women's World Cup final from one year earlier. Few doubted that these two teams were indeed the two best in the world.

Japan tested Solo throughout the entire gold-medal game. It could have been a blowout against some goalies. But not against Solo. The United States held a narrow 2–1 lead in the 83rd minute. That's when Solo faced her biggest test yet.

US defender and team captain Christie Rampone rarely makes mistakes. But suddenly she made a crucial error. Japan forward Mana Iwabuchi stole the ball just outside the left corner of the US penalty box. US defender Becky Sauerbrunn raced to cut off Iwabuchi. But the Japan forward seemed to have all

SWITCHING SIDES

Hope Solo was a great scorer in high school. She netted 109 goals as a striker for Richland High School in Washington. But University of Washington coach Lesle Gallimore recruited Solo to play goalie. "Hope was able to stop shots that most kids her age weren't," Gallimore said. "But it was also how she used her feet. The way she moved. She was one of the better athletes I'd ever seen." Her background as a field player helped her understand what opposing players were doing offensively. That made it easier for Solo to react and break up scoring chances.

the time she wanted as she entered the box.

Solo was the last line of defense. She took her position by the near post. She crouched, pumping her feet up and down quickly. She was ready to pounce. And when Iwabuchi released a powerful right-footed shot, Solo did just that.

Iwabuchi drilled her shot from around 10 yards (9.1 m) out and a few yards wide of the goal. The curling shot was right on target. It was heading toward the net at the far post.

Solo leaped to her left as soon as Iwabuchi struck the ball. Flying through the air with outstretched arms, she blocked the ball with both hands. As the ball rolled away near the end line at the far post, Solo jumped back up and took her position at that post. But a US defender was now in control of the ball. The US lead was intact. And a few minutes later, the whistle blew. The United States had won another Olympic gold medal.

"I knew I had to make the save," Solo said. "That was pretty much my only thought. I had to make that save."

American players and fans have gotten used to amazing saves like that from Solo. "You can't go without saying that Hope saved the day," US forward Abby Wambach said. "Literally. Five times."

Solo had showcased her skills on the world stage before. She first became the starting goalie for the US team in 2005. She played every minute of every US game at the 2008 Olympic Games.

"She's already an all-around athlete," 2008 US Olympic coach Phil Wheddon said. "She's got exceptional jumping ability, she's quick, and she's very explosive and powerful."

US goalie Hope Solo makes a diving save against Japan during the gold-medal game at the 2012 Olympic Games in London.

Then she starred again at the 2011 Women's World Cup. Her performance in 2011 made people take notice. Solo won the Golden Glove Award as the best goalkeeper of the tournament. She also won the Bronze Ball. That is given to the third best player of the tournament. Solo became the first goalie chosen as a top-three player at a Women's World Cup.

Guarding the Goal

The goalie has an important role. She is the last line of defense on any soccer team. It is her job to stop shots, any way she can. And unlike other soccer players, that includes stopping the ball with her hands and arms.

The casual fan might not have noticed everything that went into Solo's save against Japan. First there was positioning. Solo immediately cut off the angle by moving to the near post. Then she prepared herself for the shot. So she got low and stayed light on her feet. That allowed her to react immediately when Iwabuchi kicked the ball.

Solo jumped completely into the air when she dove. Her body was parallel to the ground. And as she dove, she kept her hands together. That made sure they were strong enough to stop the powerful shot. And when the shot hit her hands squarely, Solo was able to guide the rebound down the end line. Had the ball rebounded in front of the goal, Japan might have had another scoring opportunity.

It takes lots of practice to make saves like that. Technique is important. So is reaction and confidence. Goalies need to know exactly when to start their dive or to charge a player on a breakaway. Of course goalies also need to have great athleticism. Solo was able to spring up and fly through the air to make that save.

Solo's save made the highlight reels. But there is so much more that goes into goalkeeping for an entire game. Goalies also must be leaders of the defense. Since the goalie is in the back, she usually has the best view of the field. So she is in charge of directing her teammates to open areas or to unmarked players.

US goalie Hope Solo gets into position to try to make a stop against Canada's Christine Sinclair during their 2012 Olympic semifinal game.

Quick Tip: Reaching New Heights

Hope Solo has excellent range in goal. But she worked hard to get it. One of the drills she does with the national team is called a "depth jump with ball." She begins by standing on a box or platform approximately 2 feet (0.61 m) off the ground. She steps off the box, landing with her feet shoulder-width apart and her toes pointed forward. As she's hitting the ground, a person standing a few feet in front of her tosses a ball in the air over her head. Solo immediately explodes off the ground and taps the ball back to the thrower. The drill helps increase vertical jump height and improves reaction time and hand-eye coordination.

Goalies are also important on offense. Any time a goalie makes a save and holds on to the ball, the possession changes. That is also true when the opposing team kicks the ball out of bounds across the end line for a goal kick. So the goalie has to make the first play in a counter attack. On a goal kick she has to decide if she wants to kick the ball short or far. A short kick is often safer. However, a long kick can push the offense up the field faster. The goalie has to make the same decisions after a save. Rolling or throwing the ball to a nearby teammate is safe. Or she can punt the ball as far as she can. Whatever she decides often sets the tone for a counter attack.

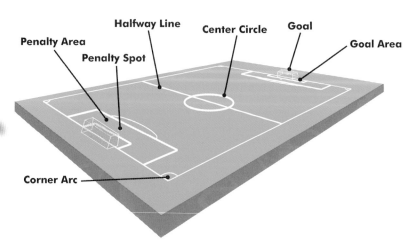

center circle

> Kickoffs take place in the center of this area. Only two players from the kicking team can be in the center circle during a kickoff.

corner arc

> The spot from which a corner kick must be taken.

goal area

> The area from which a goal kick must be taken.

penalty area

> The area of the field in which goalies can use their hands. It is also called the penalty box.

penalty spot

> The point from which a penalty shot must be taken.

assist
> A pass that leads directly to a goal.

corner kick
> A free kick from the corner awarded to the attacking team when the defending team plays the ball over its own end line.

counter attack
> Quickly changing from defense to offense.

dribbling
> Small kicks used to keep control of the ball.

extra time
> Two 15-minute periods that are played when a winner cannot be determined in regular time.

free kicks
> When a player gets to kick the ball from the spot of a foul without being guarded.

plant
> To put a foot firmly on the ground.

rebound
> When the ball bounces off something, usually a goalie, to produce another scoring chance for the offense.

save
> To stop the ball from going in the goal.

spontaneity
> Randomness.

through pass
> A pass into an open space where a teammate will soon be.

Selected Bibliography

Crisfield, Deborah W. *The Everything Kids' Soccer Book: Rules, techniques, and more about your favorite sport!* Avon, MA: Adams Media Corp., 2009.

"FIFA BALLON D'OR 2012." *FIFA.com*. FIFA. n.d. Web. 6 March 2013.

"U.S. Women." U.S. Soccer. U.S. Soccer. n.d. Web. 6 March 2013.

Further Readings

Cox, Alexander. *How to Soccer: a step-by-step guide to mastering the skills.* New York: DK, 2011.

Lennox, James W. *Soccer Skills and Drills.* Champaign, IL: Human Kinetics, 2006.

Lisi, Clemente A. *The U.S. Women's Soccer Team: An American Success Story.* Plymouth, UK: Scarecrow Press, Inc., 2010.

Ross, Dev. *Soccer!* Illus: David Wenzel. Novato, CA: Treasure Bay, Inc. 2010.

For More Information

Web Links

To learn more about soccer, visit ABDO Publishing Company online at **www.abdopublishing.com**. Web sites about soccer are featured on our Book Links page. These links are routinely monitored and updated to provide the most current information available.

Places to Visit

Home Depot Center
18400 Avalon Boulevard
Carson, CA 90746
(310) 630-2000
www.homedepotcenter.com

This field is a favorite of the US women's national team, as it hosts opponents from all over the world each year. Located on the campus of California State University, Dominguez Hills, it is also home to two men's Major League Soccer teams, the Los Angeles Galaxy and Chivas USA.

National Sports Center
1700 105th Ave. NE
Blaine, MN 55449
(800) 535-4730
www.nscsports.org

With 48 fields, the National Sports Center is recognized as the largest soccer complex in the world. Many youth soccer games and tournaments take place here each year, notably the USA Cup, which is considered the largest youth soccer tournament in the western hemisphere.

Index

ABOUT THE AUTHOR

Alex Monnig is a freelance journalist from St. Louis, Missouri. He graduated with his master's degree from the University of Missouri in May 2010. During his career he has spent time covering sporting events around the world, including the 2008 Olympic Games in China, the 2010 Commonwealth Games in India, and the 2011 Rugby World Cup in New Zealand.